S0-BCW-194

www.finishinglinepress.com

Rookland

poems by

Jesse Minkert

Finishing Line Press
Georgetown, Kentucky

Rookland

Copyright © 2017 by Jesse Minkert
ISBN 978-1-63534-268-0 First Edition
All rights reserved under International and Pan-American Copyright Conventions.
No part of this book may be reproduced in any manner whatsoever without written
permission from the publisher, except in the case of brief quotations embodied in critical
articles and reviews.

ACKNOWLEDGMENTS

"Album" first appeared in *Soundings East*, Fall 2014.
"Autopsy" first appeared in *The Limestone Journal*, 2013, and then in *Pontoon-Floating Bridge* Review #7.
"Certain Future" first appeared in *Glass: A Journal of Poetry* Volume Six Issue Two, 2014.
"Club Girl" first appeared in *Aunt Chloe* 2011.
"Collin Washes his Hands" first appeared in *The Minetta Review*'s Fall 2013 Issue.
"Harvest of Marrow" and "Misalignment" first appeared in the graphic poetry chapbook, *RAFT,* 2014.
"Her Own Concoction" first appeared in *DMQ Review*, Winter 2015.
"Incursion" first appeared in the *Licking River Review*, Winter 2012/Spring 2013.
"Leather Seat Cushion" first appeared in *The Cape Rock*, Spring 2014.
"Millwright" first appeared in *The Manhattanville Review*, 2014
"Mouth of the Sea" first appeared in *Caveat Lector*, Spring 2013.
"Outdoor Concert" first appeared in *Mount Hope* 3, Spring 2013
"Rainbow Face" first appeared in *The Georgetown Review*, 2014-2015.
"Love Dog" first appeared in *The Wandering Hermit Review*, Winter/Spring 2006
"Sylvia's Hair" first appeared in *Raven Chronicles*, Spring 2004.
"Untidy Enterprise" first appeared in *The Free State Review*, 2014.

Publisher: Leah Maines

Editor: Christen Kincaid

Cover Art: J. Gary Minkert, minkert.weebly.com

Author Photo: Jack Straw Cultural Center, photographer Sherwin Eng.

Cover Design: Elizabeth Maines McCleavy

Printed in the USA on acid-free paper.
Order online: www.finishinglinepress.com
also available on amazon.com

Author inquiries and mail orders:
Finishing Line Press
P. O. Box 1626
Georgetown, Kentucky 40324
U. S. A.

Table of Contents

FEET IN BOTH WORLDS

The crown tonight weighs heavy on Her Majesty's white curls.
Her feet are tired, neck stiff and sore, and a paper cut
got from a page in a diplomatic document
throbs on her thumb. This communiqué recounts:
the Heir Apparent, with an underage companion,
sped from a party in a roadster with a faulty brake.
Collision with a tree ensued, as had doctors, police, journalists.

She summoned and dispatched the handlers. She'd now
just as soon smear the problem into daylight
on cleansing fingers of sleep, but a box of chocolate licorice,
two double grande cappuccinos, and visions of tabloid
headlines have banished her from that frontier.

When she was but a child, her huntsmen beat the brush.
Hares and vixens ran for her diversion, but tonight
coachmen lie abed with scullery wenches. Percheron mares
snort in their stalls. Valets in their nightshirts
and ladies in their flimsy sleeping gowns don't hear
her pacing barefoot through the galleries.

Her Majesty paws about in the fridge. What, in this plastic tub,
have we, two-day-old lasagna? Yes, but we think not.
Remains of a deli rotisserie chicken? Likely neither that.

Aha! A half-devoured tub of bread pudding. She fumbles
for the drier rack and grasps a spoon. In the Royal Chamber
the Prince Consort has gathered all the covers 'round him. Digital
red numbers shift from three fifty-nine to four double naught.

Her Majesty props her back on pillows, slips her glasses
onto her nose, thumbs the clip-on reading lamp,
and opens her paperback cozy to the corner-bent page.

HER OWN CONCOCTION

Melanie weaves a few blades of grass
into three-winged spinners and ties them
onto dandelion stalks with fern-leaf
spiders' webs. They drift on the breeze
above the grassy park until
these murderous gossamer lures
tangle on the wings of zebra moths
who writhe their last gasps on seats
of swings. She gathers them,
mashes them to a paste in her pestle,
stirs them into her hot chocolate milk
and sips until she feels
that flutter in her throat.

CLUB GIRL

Her thrustulating hips and arms
thump and bump to the hip-hop queen
the way her mother did as Janis
offered up another bit of her heart,
and grandma gave Elvis
whatever he called out for,
and the way great grannie swung
to the boogie-woogie accents;
slippered and sliding eight to the bar,
and great great gramma
with her long, long legs,
back in the twenties;
her knees and elbows flew
to the tunes that flared out
from the bells of trumpets
like a crown of lilies pinned to the head
of a New Orleans dance hall queen.

ALBUM

On this page Belinda is laughing with friends,
arms around her waist, every pair of lips open,
teeth blazing in the light of the flash.
She leans too far to keep upright on her own.
Collin is in back, face as flat as the day
he dug a grave for his dog.

But here they stand beside each other
on the street. The city's dressed
in a pelt of ice. Tire tracks calligraph
the road. Belinda huddles in her hood,
squinting from her capsule; Collin,
hands in pockets, bends his head,
face lost in the shadow of his parka.

Look at our Belinda solo now, sitting
at a table dented by a thousand pitchers,
her plaid scarf on her neck, her white sweater,
the ragged hole at the elbow,
beer foam in her glass, mouth parted,
hair pulled back but for a single strand
dangling in front of a half-closed eye.

Who's this figure in the foreground,
the balding, uncombed head, rounded
shoulders, a hand in a dark sleeve,
fingers clutching another tumbler of beer?

MILLWRIGHT

Optical motion sensors
display two thousand fantasies
two thousand times a minute.
Two thousand automatic tongues
lick two thousand labels and
two thousand automatic thumbs
smooth them to the vessels
wherein his visions, with
muted squeals and giggles
splash and bask as if on
an outing to the lake.

Robot arms extend.
Stainless hands with
rubber fingerprints lift
and drop the vessels
into cardboard cases.
A shuddering conveyor,
stacks on stacks on palettes
in a warehouse mind.

The millwright's lips,
sculpted as if in clay,
nest on a pillow, flutter and snore,
a noise like a window fan
with a stuttering blade.

LA GIOCONDA

Walking on the path Greta finds a child
half-buried in the ground.
His plump arms and legs kick and flail.
His eyes clench shut; his nostrils flare.

Greta has turned eleven today.
Her mother served her
low-fat cake and ice cream.
She couldn't not allude to Greta's weight.
"Exercise is good," she said.
"Go take a walk outside."

The child's face like a smudged bubble rises from the dirt.
His belly pushes above the twigs and pebbles.

Greta wears the denim jumper
that her sister had outgrown a year ago.
It fits her poorly. All clothes fit her poorly.

Six months from this day, Greta's layers
of fat will melt. She will need bras.
She will monthly bleed.

The toddler pushes out from the earth
wobbles to his feet. His green eyes turn to Greta.

He studies her the way a tourist in the Louvre
studies the Mona Lisa, unable to blink or look away,
desperate to decipher the consequence of what he sees.

MISALIGNMENT

The tapestry has a square cut out
where Mrs. Capuchin had sat
at tea with Marv the constrictor.
The sun is up. At least that much.

Between Marv's aching jaws,
Mrs. Capuchin's a plausible
morsel to savor, yet he fits
his tongue to the master lock
and answers her with gauzy
courtesy, as if a spider's web
were wrapped around a fist,

but Mrs. Cap still hesitates
to recite her pantomime
after all that shuffle and shock.
It's just enough to make her drowse,
even in places like here,
where the child careens a truck,
or here, where the father falls down
and wets himself laughing.

COLLIN WASHES HIS HANDS

Trenches of soot and grease in the maps of his palms,
Intractable life nestles in his pores
eager to sink its tiny jaws into his meat.
Spiders' carcasses, broken roaches' legs,
smears of mucous accreted under his fingernails.

He scours his cuticles, knuckles, wrinkles,
flushes the bacterial mobs,
foams away the grainy ash
of meteorites and volcanoes,
scrubs off the scampering itches
who seek new crevices, new shelter
from the brush's bristles' onslaught.

But what he labors to cleanse is not this hide,
more the dread that he might awaken
from his relentless conjectures of whom
he can assume will conquer him, and when.

BOTTLE OF OFFAL

Ya shoot that doe from the road,
drag it to the pickup, heave it in the bed.
In the garage ya cut the venison
off the carcass, and the rest ya grind,
yeah, grind it all down,
liver kidneys spleen feet brain.
Grind it 'til it runs like ooze
from an infected toenail.

Simmer in a pot for forty days
'til the evil in it rises,
cut with grain alcohol,
pour into an old, cold green bottle,
and hammer the punctured cork
back in the mouth.

Now ya get ya punk kid brother drunk.
Show 'im the bottle. Bet 'im a twenty
he can't chug it down. Watch 'im try.
He hurls it back out on the floor
'cause he's a soft little Momma's sweetie-pie,
and he'll be NOTHING MORE FOREVER.

OUTDOOR CONCERT

Bennie finds his zipper stuck
between the Bosporus
and the Anasazi home

have mercy in the clarinets
have moisture on the reeds
keys move up and down
according to whim and wind.

Bennie pulls hard
to close the distance
what seems close
is married to the map
and can't betray the inches
that chatter up the ridgeline.

Brass blows sassy
from the high back row
wait for word from Bennie
what follows in the interval.

Silt gags the Bosporus.
Gone the Anasazi.
Ladders bowls windows
show whom they were
to families from Hokkaido.

The timpani the snares
the high hats tremble.
Teeth in the final outburst realign
compel Bennie to sing
to badgers as to brothers.

INCURSION

Our papa wears those tapered slacks
that bind where compass points refuse to close.
The passing throng throws candy cigarettes
to bodies asleep in doorways.

Mama puts red pennies on her pillow to pacify
her sleep. Accelerant collects between the slats.
In the glass a dispatch to the squadrons.

Fire marches on the hill. Grasses thirst
for a blink's worth of purification.
A bell in the distance, the colonels fleeing.

They've sent us kids to Cleveland for the winter
there to confer with the brigadier until the saviors
drop from passing planes in multiples of twenty.

HARVEST OF MARROW

The old man, feet among the roots,
should have learnt by now
to carry his bones one atop the other.

"These knots," he says, "that harden
on my bones don't help me listen
to the saxophones. This ravaged
hand stings from the salt. Blood
on the strand purples the asphalt.

My mouth fills now with rain,
and now with wind,
with soil and coins, wasps'
wings, shouts, splinters,
threads of socks, scraps of skin."

Bones sound, when they shatter,
like celery sticks between
the fingers of his daughter
who's prepared the tray of ranch,
bleu cheese, or hummus dips,
but his crushing teeth can smell
his skeleton moving
between the millstones
of the world's mastication.

UNEVEN SILHOUETTE

Shadows hurry. The night turns gray as his armored particles
migrate to his unraveled edges as if called, as if threatened.

Discord on the plaza smears across cobblestones like marmalade.
Windows shatter. Burning clouds drift past the lampposts.

He clutches at his knees in the closet under the stairs,
the dark sweet corner where the slant of the wall turns in.

Distant quick reports outside. A dripping awning contours
a wet edge on the walk. Heels tap on concrete.

Her cape is black; hair like rusty water curling in the gutter.
Her outline snaps into focus, then blurs inside the curtains.

Bleached figures stagger in the avenues. Fading slogans
dissipate the drama, the scene now shrunken, desiccated.

Lights go out for prime time curfew. Pockets of shadow
fold over the streets. Thoroughfares sound hollow.

Branches whisper to the current of air. Dirt swirls
like hordes of devils above the vacant fields of play.

She finds him on the carpet, features smudged, snoring
through the final act, She shakes his shoulder. Eyelids part.

It's over, she says. Nobody dead today. But what, he shudders,
put such hard callouses over the rage?

LOVE DOG

On their third date Dave told Carol the story of Linda and the dog.

Linda's dog was always right there.

It was big.

It was black and hairy.

Its teeth were long and yellow.

Linda thought it was cute.

The dog was in love with Dave.

When Dave and Linda kissed, the dog joined in.

It slobbered all over Dave's face.

Its breath was like a sewer.

Linda gave the dog licks from her ice cream.

"A dog's mouth," said Linda, "is cleaner than a man's."

The dog jumped on the bed with Linda and Dave.

It liked to lick Dave's crotch.

It begged at the table.

Linda fed it scraps from Dave's plate.

Dave wanted to feed it steak and razor blades.

It peed in Dave's car.

Dave, when Linda wasn't looking, peed on the dog.

Linda liked to wrestle with the dog on the floor in her underwear.

Its penis was as red as a pomegranate.

Linda laughed.

Dave wondered what might be going on when he wasn't there.

Linda told Dave he was being paranoid.

Dave wanted to throw the dog from an overpass.

He wanted to drive to the country, throw a stick, and drive away.

He wanted to accidentally back his car over it.

Linda told Dave he was emotionally backward.

Dave told Linda he was allergic.

Linda told Dave he was insecure.

Dave told Linda she was bipolar.

Linda told Dave he was moody.

Dave told Linda she was walking a thin line.

Linda demanded back the key to her apartment.

Dave explained to Carol that the experience had left him deeply scarred, apprehensive, unwilling to reach out.

Carol understood perfectly because all of Linda's friends hated Linda's dog.

(Linda had introduced Carol to Dave.)

All he really wanted, Dave told Carol, their perspiration pooling beneath them on the wrinkled sheets as the dawn sun smiled through the window and warmed their feet while Carol's cockatiel squawked for its breakfast in the living room,

was love.

RAINBOW FACE

Belinda won't think about
the bruise around her eye,
not so eggplant-colored now,
fading to yellow and magenta tints.
Her friends' asking eyes and the lies
she offers them for answers
hurt as much as the hairline
fracture in her zygomatic arch.
In venues where she's not well known,
the patrons snatch a glimpse
of a collision drifting through the curtain.
They don't know what breaks
or blunt disruptions have colored
her demeanor, nor do they wish to learn.
They fold their pain inside their garments
so those with mutilations of their own
won't have to step in front of everyone
and perform a feeling.

LEATHER SEAT CUSHION

He will try to not spill his drink on the furniture,
but he will have had too many, and the stain,
oh, the stain will draw his mate's attention.
She will scold him from beyond the gaze
of casual acquaintances.

They will form the notion that he has often failed.
His lapses of judgment, focus, balance, grace,
will incur for the hostess a substantial cleaning bill.
He will offer to pay. The hostess will say,
"Accidents are normal. They happen to us all."
For these words he will fall in love with her.

But the mate will say, "Try not to mortify me
before strangers who mean more to me than you."
Now the room will know that he will be inches
from sleeping on a bug-infested bed in a motor court,
from briefcases full of briefs, from asset distributions.

Failure, failure, deeper failure than the circle
expanding on the seat of the cow skin armchair in ecru
on which the purple stands out like a bruise.
He will cry inside for that lost liquid mouthful
discoloring the tightly-stitched hide.

He will yell, "Why display our torment
to these casual acquaintances? Should they care?
Shouldn't they prefer not to see, to hear,
how much you detest me? How much
do you think I have left to feel about you?"

But even as he bellows, he will know he is lost.
He will wear the blame to bed that night.
Let me die, he will beg to the empty ether,
let me die right now on this carpeted floor
as these words stutter from between my lips.

AUTOPSY

Molecules crawl through arteries,
batteries run down.
Time becomes a battle to catch breath.
A face fixed in a plastic mask
can't remember where the air comes in.

Cold will climb bones,
close its fingers on the heart,
and maybe that annoying beat
will take this opportunity
to break its pace.

Let my children enter.
On the table in the coroner's closet
let them see the carcass.

Guide their hands into my abdomen.
Run their fingers along my vertebrae.
Here is where the cartilage has worn.
This is my vestigial tail.
On these locations ribs attach
and curl around to gather at the sternum.
The bump on the left, a meaningless imperfection
serves as another marker,
useful only to identify my vestiges.

Allow them their repulsion at this spectacle
I've performed for their sake.
My cells have discarded me.
I've become a lie
emergent from survivors' tongues.

CERAMIST

Rain drips from the canopy.
Runnels dig through patches of snow
beyond Marjorie's concrete platform.

She acquired her scar
from the fall she took in the kiln
shifting shelves, setting rows of cones.

Slip clings like cream to her fingers
to leathery swells tapers shoulders
mouths of jars cups urns jugs vases.

The kiln door shut. Gas lit. Marjorie peers
through the glass until the cones bend
like damp fabric and clay glows crimson.

Her insulating gloves unlatch the door
lift vessels from their furnace womb
into canisters packed with autumn tree fall.

Untouchable heat sets leaves aflame.
Metal covers seal out oxygen
asphyxiating hidden atmosphere.

Objects arrayed on their cooling slabs
her sleeves roll up. Gloves apron helmet drop.
Scorched broken strands of hair. Her cracked
calloused fingers brush fried ends from her collar.

Marjorie squats on her x-legged camp stool
studies the wrinkled raw exposures
skins molting shedding making naked.
Black lines murmur under the blinding luster.
Hot spots blush and shimmer in the glaze.

MOUTH OF THE SEA

"Sharks Absent, Swimmer, 64, Strokes From Cuba to Florida"
New York Times, September 2, 2013

The somnolescent giantess won't release
her grasp on the breathing membrane
separating air from sea. Pulses depart
to every point and speak in shimmers
to sheared-off dreadnoughts of ice.

One may never know her caress
but imagine instead the millennia
of sediment spilling from her hair.
Reflections of clouds, accretions by rain
and rivers, join the shifting surface.
Their songs broadcast on the ocean's radio.

She swims to Latin rhythms farther
than the measure of terrors in her wake.
Her fingers inject and stir; her breath spills out.
The surface welcomes what the deep would devour.

One may slap stomachs, play reeds
of cellophane inserted in a crease
or fold or elbow to welcome her ashore
to call her water nymph
reborn within the tide.

CRACKS ON THE RING
"THE SHUTTLE EXPLODES
6 In Crew And High School Teacher Are Killed 74 Seconds
After Liftoff"   *New York Times, January 28, 1986*

Here comes the last of the gargoyle chatter
straight out from the seal in the rim
distended as she remembered
black as the soot on the grass.

Her thin-walled colonies pursued
their natural hydraulic instinct
but the tanks were not well sealed.
Seepages at certain locations defied
all caulking guns soldering irons
gaskets layers of ribbons of tape
and heated fuel emissions
released a discontented spray.

Liquids cleared across a solution.
A cleansing separating barrier
allowed them to swim through openings
to pass exude reveal their hue.

Time disobeyed its essential duty
whispered its nebulous excuses
dredged deep trenches in her flesh
torn from sutures too wide to close.

Her organs shifted out from her torso
hung enveloped in a sheath of debris
outside that novel shuffle of material
that ovoid scatter merged and acquiesced.

Below, the basin collected a deposit
a concession a delay a perforation
folded into the starboard side.

CERTAIN FUTURE

In her tissues Jason's mother reenacts the deaths
of her ancestors: a rehearsal for his inheritance.

He studies what wakes each day in his sons
and reads in them that same destiny.

He wants to hold them close.
Every order he wants to say is perfect order.

A placement acts to expedite a replacement
but replacements suggest displacements,

imply the sweating seams
the pressures in the atmosphere.

In the bucket, sand and pretty stones
shells broken in the surf, scraps of salty wood.

In sleep he saw the Percheron mare.
Light shimmered in her mane.

More fever than dream, he told himself,
false patterns clinging to his retinas.

SYLVIA'S HAIR

is all that remains
of a lost empire of sun worshippers;
a mountain of shards,
the image of the Goddess
engraved on every piece.

is a gold-leaf crossword puzzle in Arabic,
is 52,715 palominos on locoweed;
a storm of grasshoppers choreographed by Twyla Tharp.

is the Mandelbrot Set
soaked in brandy
and set afire
with a drop of rainwater
in a loop of summer grass.

In a blur of haste, Monet's brush flickers through brilliant air,
from palette to canvas and back. The sun repositions
in the sky. Monet tosses the canvas into roadside grass,
lifts a new one from a stack. Another Monet watches
the first Monet's shadow lengthen, captures Monet's
impression, throws the image down, and starts another.
That's Sylvia's hair.

Sylvia's braids are hawsers
that lead into all of the other dimensions,
anchored to the heads of all of the other Sylvias,
keeping the Knot of All Worlds tight,
not ravelable by any set of busy fingers.

Each strand of Sylvia's hair is a twist of candle smoke.

SOUP

By this time they could only
text each other. Nights were long and empty.
Wind bashed trees against the windows.
The hands on the kitchen clock moved
stubbornly through their job.

She wrote that she had met
some very kind people.
She hadn't told them everything.
He lied to her; he said he got a haircut,
was working, eating healthy food,
cutting back on beer and cigarettes.

He wouldn't have been surprised
if the very kind people were inventions.
He kept his phone in his overcoat,
took it out to read her messages
as he sipped his cup of salty soup.

UNTIDY ENTERPRISE

That damp and dirty sliced up the middle T-shirt
in that torn brown grocery bag stank like lemons
smeared on a pine tree. Nothing else close at hand
to sop the blood.

You opened that valve and let it surge,
let the sheets coagulate below,
saw the rooks fly in from Rookland.

You passed the test, slept through the worst
of the screaming, kept your name a cipher
even in the face of the family.

You buried the evidence far from the trail,
rinsed away the clots, tried to forget
how they felt clinging to your fingers.

The rooks assemble in the trees, wings and tails
glistening in the downing sun. Dark won't serve
as remedy from this grisly venture.

Congratulations, Timmy. You've found
a disappearing place good enough to last
until the rooks snatch your spoor from the wind.

Now sharpen the sticks. Double wrap the tape
around the dressings. Their calls are coming closer.

J esse **Minkert**'s father taught art classes in their home town in Texas. Jesse was one of his first students at the age of twelve. He now has a BFA as a painter and an MA as a sculptor. Between the two degrees was a gap of eleven years during which he worked as a sign painter, a picture framer, a foundry patternmaker, a wood carver, a hot tub installer, and other jobs. He moved to Seattle and developed diabetic retinopathy, a major cause of blindness. His vision survived, and he began working on arts access for blind and visually impaired people. In 1991 Minkert founded and still serves as Executive Director of Arts and Visually Impaired Audiences. His new path moved him toward writing plays for theater and radio, then into poems, short stories and novels. He served on the board of the Red Sky Poetry Theatre. In 2008, Wood Works published his letterpress chapbook, *Shortness of Breath & Other Symptoms*. His work has appeared in over fifty journals and collections including *Caveat Lector, Common Knowledge, Confrontation, Cream City Review, Floating Bridge Review, Georgetown Review, Harpur Palate, The Minetta Review, Mount Hope,* and *Poetry Northwest*. He is a 2016 Pushcart nominee. Each summer for twenty years Minkert has worked with the Jack Straw Cultural Center to help visually impaired school kids perform and produce radio plays and PSAs from original scripts.

CPSIA information can be obtained
at www.ICGtesting.com
Printed in the USA
LVOW11s1217290717
542835LV00001B/33/P

9 781635 342680